Retail Rhapsody

A HAIKU COLLECTION

M.J. FIFIELD

ILLUSTRATIONS BY HEATHER R. HOLDEN

FAVORITE SPOON PUBLISHING

Copyright © 2025 by Favorite Spoon Publishing, LLC

All Rights Reserved. This book or any portion thereof may not be reproduced or used in any manner whatsoever without the express written permission of the publisher except for the use of brief quotations in a book review.

Printed in the United States of America
First Printing, 2025

ISBN: 978-0-9961074-8-8

Favorite Spoon Publishing
1720 Malabar Road #500509
Malabar, FL 32950

Illustrations: Heather R. Holden; www.uniquelyholden.com

Also by M.J. Fifield

Effigy
Second Nature
Love & Other Lies

For the co-workers and customers who inspired this book.

I couldn't have done it without you.

CONTENTS

Introduction	*xi*
Customer Service	1
Co-Workers	35
Management	51
The Breakroom	79
My Actual Job	91
Acknowledgements	125
About the Author	127

INTRODUCTION

ONCE UPON A TIME, I worked in retail. I was employed by a variety of companies in a variety of positions, from entry-level to management. Mostly, however, I worked in the stock room and assisted on the sales floor whenever needed. I was *extremely* good at my job, which I feel is important to note here and now for reasons that will soon become obvious.

One slow day when I had done all there was to do and was subsequently bored out of my mind, I decided to write about my day in haiku form, just to see if I could.

Turns out, I could.

And thus, an obsession was born.

A haiku, in the event that you're unfamiliar with it, is a three-lined poem which originated in Japan around the seventeenth century. The first and third lines traditionally contain five syllables each, and the second line has seven, for a total of seventeen syllables. (Yes, there is a 3-5-3 format as well as some, in my humble opinion, nonsense about short poems without a set syllable count being American haiku, and to each their own, I suppose, but all the poems found in this book utilize the 5-7-5 format.) The subject matter is customarily a fleeting moment in nature.

I, however, decided to write about a fleeting moment (as well as some not-so fleeting moments) in retail.

Here now, compiled for your reading pleasure, is a collection of those (possibly *slightly* sarcastic) haiku I wrote during my many years in retail. Each poem represents an absolutely true experience and my true feelings dealing with those true experiences.

To protect the innocent (and, perhaps, the not-so innocent) no names of companies, co-workers, bosses, or customers are mentioned.

I hope you enjoy reading them as much as I enjoyed writing them.

Retail Rhapsody

CUSTOMER
SERVICE

PUBLIC SERVICE ANNOUNCEMENT

The customers are
the worst part of working in
customer service.

You're not always right.
Just thought that should be stated
before we begin.

I hate those moments
when customers are correct.
Sets bad precedent.

But fortunately,
it doesn't happen often.
Thank goodness for that.

FEIGNED INTEREST

I hate my work voice.
It makes me sound much nicer
than I really am.

"How are you today?"
I ask with a fake smile,
but inside I cringe.

Here's the thing, shoppers:
I don't care about your day.
They just make me ask.

I'M NOT THE SALES ASSOCIATE YOU'RE LOOKING FOR

When customers ask
if I work here, I always
want to answer no.

Customer asks me,
"Excuse me, do you work here?"
Depends why you ask.

Attention shoppers:
Yes, I could help you with that.
I just don't want to.

TO CATCH AN OBVIOUS THIEF

Customer asks me
if he can steal some clothing.
That's not how it works.

What is wrong with you?
Wait until my back is turned,
then just have at it.

This place doesn't pay
enough for me to worry
about stopping you.

FITTING ROOM FAIL

Customer confused
fitting room for a bathroom.
A job for my boss.

Fitting rooms are for
the trying-on of clothing.
They are not toilets.

The worst part is this
isn't even the first time
someone has done this.

I SEE NAKED PEOPLE

See customers strip
in the middle of the store.
How I love this job.

So many people
running around half-naked.
What's happening here?

What is it about
this place that makes you forget
how to put on clothes?

UP CLOSE AND TOO PERSONAL

Customer asks me
to check the size of her pants
while she's wearing them.

Sure, I'd love to look
down your pants to check the size.
Thought you'd never ask.

It's not like we have
these special rooms where you could
do that on your own.

NOT YOUR BIOGRAPHER

That moment when a
customer corners you to
tell her life's story.

That's really nice, ma'am,
but I actually have
other things to do.

You didn't notice,
but I'm the lone employee
here to help shoppers.

I SEE MORE NAKED PEOPLE

For crying out loud,
the fitting room doors do close.
Feel free to try it.

Beware of the store,
where all customers will lose
all inhibitions.

At least you're stripping
in a fitting room and not
out on the sales floor.

I need a job that
has fewer naked people
asking me for help.

MY FAULT FOR ANSWERING THE PHONE

This guy on the phone
wants me to describe all the
pants we have for men.

Sure. It's not like I
have anything else to do
while I'm here today.

Could you possibly
narrow down what kind of pant
you are looking for?

No? Okay, let's see…
We have pants for hiking and
biking and jogging.

STILL MY FAULT FOR ANSWERING THE PHONE

Cargo, corduroy,
dress trousers, carpenter pants,
chinos and denim.

Do any of those
strike your fancy in the least,
or should I go on?

We also carry
a variety of shorts.
Should I run through those?

The guy then hangs up,
and now I will never know
what pants he wanted.

MAYBE THERE ARE *SOME* STUPID QUESTIONS

A customer calls
to ask if we'll be well-stocked
Black Friday weekend.

No, we'll only have
three T-shirts in the whole store.
Better come early.

It is the biggest
shopping weekend of the year.
What do you think, ma'am?

DOWNRIGHT RUDE

A man says to me,
"You can't be in charge because
you are a woman."

"Everybody knows
women can't be managers.
Too emotional."

Sighing, I reply,
"I'm sorry you feel that way,
you sexist jackass."

Being written up
for saying 'sexist jackass'.
I regret nothing.

COMPLIMENT?

Woman wants to know
what size I wear because I'm
about her friend's size.

"You're a skinny bitch
just like her," the woman says.
"That's a compliment."

"It sure sounded like
a compliment," I reply.
"Bet your friend agrees."

MENOPAUSE MOMENTS

Spent thirty minutes
talking with a customer
about menopause.

Cool. Thanks for sharing.
Maybe I could help you find
some T-shirts or pants?

LAST-MINUTE ~~PEST~~ GUEST

Customer comes in
just as the store is closing.
Are you kidding me?

Sure. Come on in, ma'am.
It's not like I wanted to
go home or something.

Absolutely, ma'am,
please try on every last coat
we have in the place.

This definitely
couldn't have waited until
another damn day.

LAST-MINUTE ~~PEST~~ GUEST
(CONTINUED)

Hey, just so you know,
we closed ten minutes ago,
but please take your time.

The only thing I
like more than working here is
having to stay late.

I hope you're planning
to spend a lot of money
before you head out.

And you leave without
buying a single item.
Totally worth it.

BLACK FRIDAY BONANZA

It is four a.m.
Lines of shoppers wait outside.
Must be Black Friday.

Do they even know
how much this sale really sucks?
It's so not worth it.

The whole store's on sale.
You don't need to keep asking
if things are on sale.

I've walked ten miles
this Black Friday shift so far.
Three hours to go…

BLACK FRIDAY BONANZA
(CONTINUED)

Black Friday shopping
is seriously the worst.
Wall-to-wall people.

People trash the store,
then wonder why they can't find
what they're looking for.

Looking at a mound
of jumbled-up T-shirts and
trying not to scream.

Let me put away
that unwanted shirt for you.
You'll just do it wrong.

BLACK FRIDAY BONANZA
(CONTINUED)

So many shoppers
complaining about the sale.
Go shop somewhere else.

I do not control
what the company decides
to mark down each year.

Day after Christmas
is equally just as bad.
Why must people suck?

All right, you caught me.
I'll take you out back where we
keep the secret sale.

BLACK FRIDAY BONANZA
(CONTINUED)

Day comes to an end.
Doors are locked, music turned off.
Store is a trash pit.

Associates weep
as clean-up efforts begin.
This will take all night.

Shoppers will only
destroy everything again
tomorrow morning.

This is how it goes
when you're working in retail.
The circle of life.

ABOVE MY PAY GRADE

Customer wants me
to change return policy.
He doesn't like it.

Oh, no problem, sir.
I'll just call Corporate and
push that through for you.

The minimum-wage
stock girl definitely has
that ability.

PDA

A couple's getting
frisky in the fitting room.
At least the door's closed.

Resisting the urge
to knock and ask if they need
any help in there.

It would be wrong to
applaud when they come out, right?
Asking for a friend…

NICE PEOPLE DO EXIST

Helping nice people
in the fitting rooms today.
Forgot they exist.

It is a pleasure
to help people when they're nice.
Doesn't happen much.

I'd be happy to
fetch another size for you
because you're polite.

NICE PEOPLE DO EXIST
(CONTINUED)

You have said please and
you haven't yelled at me for
things that aren't my fault.

You haven't asked me
to look down your pants or shirt.
That's always a plus.

Please have a nice day.
I sincerely mean that, too.
I more often don't.

TALES FROM THE TENT SALE

It's tent sale weekend!
Come dig through the product that
no one wants to buy!

Need an ugly shirt?
We have 500 of them.
Get 'em while you can!

Or just wait until
next year's tent sale comes around.
They'll still be here then.

GOOD WILL SHOPPER

Guy wants to return
a pair of shorts that he bought
at the Goodwill Store.

Maybe you could try
going back to the store where
you bought the damn shorts?

RETURN OF THE NICE CUSTOMERS

The nice customers
return to bring me cookies
as thanks for my help.

Ha! See, management?
I can totally be nice
when I want to be.

AND THEN THERE'S THIS GUY

Man harassing me
because he doesn't like the
price of a jacket.

You can keep being
an asshole to me, but it
won't change anything.

Might I suggest that
if you don't like the prices
you shop somewhere else?

He finally leaves,
claiming he'll never return.
Sounds good to me, sir.

KINDNESS BACKFIRE

A customer wants
to give me a hug because
I was so helpful.

Thanks for the offer,
but I don't even like to
hug people I know.

BEST OF THE REST

There's a gentleman
who keeps calling me 'sweetie'.
That shows what he knows.

Creepy customer
just won't stop staring at me.
Can I help you, sir?

Shoppers are being
extremely obtuse today.
Can't take anymore.

Attention shoppers:
The stock girl will lose her mind
if you don't leave now.

CO-WORKERS

SHINY HAPPY PEOPLE

My co-workers are
far too chipper this morning.
Something must be done.

Why are you happy?
Don't you know this is the place
where happiness dies?

I need a donut.
I may smother co-workers
if I don't get one.

WATERCOOLER TALK

Another shift brings
another discussion of
boss's cellulite.

I don't understand
why my co-workers want to
discuss this so much.

Basho never wrote
haiku about cellulite.
I envy him that.

HELP NOT WANTED

For the love of God,
back away slowly and stop
touching everything.

No, you can't help me.
You will only do it wrong.
Please don't even try.

It's easier if
I do everything myself
and you go away.

JUST HOW WRONG IS MURDER, EXACTLY?

What the hell happened
to my neat and clean stockroom?
Heads are gonna roll…

Co-workers destroyed
all of yesterday's hard work.
I can't kill them, right?

My stockroom is trashed,
and my co-workers wonder
why I'm so damn mad.

THE NEW GUY

Why is the new guy
so damn happy and perky?
Oh, that's right. He's new.

New guy says to me,
"So, are you having fun yet?"
Please don't be that guy.

What the hell, new guy?
Are you perhaps confused by
what 'go away' means?

Did they tell you that
annoying me was part of
your job description?

THE NEW GIRL

New girl left a list
of work for me to complete.
What's happening here?

Attention new girl:
I leave you work; you do it.
That's how your job works.

Don't leave lists for me.
I won't do them and they will
only piss me off.

THE NEW GIRL
(CONTINUED)

One more thing, new girl:
We don't carry 'otterwear'.
Please learn how to spell.

Also, you should stop
rearranging stockroom shelves.
I do not like it.

Damn, you're annoying.
I hope these are your Triscuits
that I'm now eating.

GAMES PEOPLE PLAY

The topic today:
How long will the new guy last?
Please place your bets now!

Someone else has quit,
and the boss won't tell us who…
Speculation starts.

Employees begin
game to guess which one of us
will quit our job next.

I'm surprised to say
I am not the odds-on fave
in the betting pool.

I CAN'T EVEN

Co-worker says he
wants to be tazed and maced for
the experience.

He saw it online
and now he wants to try it.
I am so perplexed.

He likes spicy foods,
so he thinks he can take mace
without much trouble.

There are just no words
for my feelings at this time
except…WHAT THE HELL?!?

OOPS...MY BAD

Accidentally
threw a box at co-worker.
Didn't see him there.

I'm so sorry, man.
I wouldn't have thrown that box
if I had seen you.

I actually
really like working with you.
Will you forgive me?

MEMORANDUM

To my co-workers:
You may request my help, but
you won't demand it.

I don't work for you,
so please don't act otherwise.
It will not end well.

You think I'm mean now?
Wait and see what happens if
you do this again.

KEEPS ME HUMBLE

Co-worker asks me
if I am rich and famous
because I write books.

Oh yeah—I am quite
the rich and famous author.
That's why I work here.

And Stephen King works
the overnight shift at the
7-11.

BEST OF THE REST

Co-worker brought me
chocolate donuts today.
I like her so much.

I would like to punch
my co-worker in the face.
More than once, even.

My co-workers seem
to be terrified of me.
Wonder why that is.

MANAGEMENT

HERO POSE(R)

Behold management—
standing proudly at the front,
watching her domain.

With hands on her hips,
she sees everything and does
nothing about it.

HERE'S THE DEAL

Every time my boss
asks me how to do their job,
I ask for a raise.

I will happily
tell you what you want to know
once you have done that.

Think it's only fair
that if I'm doing your job
I get paid for it.

If you don't like that,
you could always learn how to
do your job yourself.

WE'LL SEE ABOUT THAT

Boss says I'm perfect.
Strange she won't remember when
I'm due for a raise.

My boss claims she will
never ever fire me.
Challenge accepted.

GO-TO GIRL

Boss called me her girl?
I hate to break it to her,
but the hell I am.

I don't want to be
your go-to girl anymore.
Please find someone else.

NICE TRY

My boss told me no.
Adorable how he thinks
that I might listen.

On paper, you're boss,
but it's better if you don't
tell me what to do.

Micromanaging
pisses me right the hell off.
Please stop doing it.

I CAN'T MAKE THIS STUFF UP

Boss just called to say
her clothes aren't dry yet, so she's
going to be late.

New boss has gone home,
citing a panic attack.
She won't last long here.

Boss won't stop talking
about *Dancing With the Stars*.
Someone kill me now.

BRIBES, PART ONE

Oh, dear manager,
I can't be bribed with candy.
Try brownies instead.

You cannot bribe me
with a Boston cream donut.
Maybe a dozen?

WATCHING THE CLOCK, PART ONE

In the parking lot,
waiting to see which boss will
show up late today.

If I showed up late
as frequently as they do,
I'd be written up.

How late does your boss
have to be before you are
allowed to go home?

REGRETS, PART ONE

My boss has announced
that he is sick of this place.
Get in line, buddy.

We all hate our job.
Please cry about it elsewhere.
I'm trying to work.

I don't have the time
nor desire to indulge
your temper tantrum.

MONKEY BUSINESS

My boss is proof that
a poorly trained monkey could
succeed at this job.

Now I feel I should
make amends to the monkey
for that last haiku.

So sorry, monkey,
you did nothing to deserve
that comparison.

NAP TIME

My boss is napping
on the stockroom shelves today.
When is my nap time?

Must resist the urge
to draw on my boss's face
while she is sleeping.

Boss is still sleeping.
I want to write a haiku,
but I'm too damn mad.

STOLEN MOTIVATION

Boss stole the credit
for the sale that I worked for.
I'm so glad I tried.

Boss insinuates
I lack the motivation
to help customers.

Huh. That is so weird.
I cannot imagine why
that would be the case.

WATCHING THE CLOCK, PART TWO

Sitting outside store,
waiting for my boss to show.
How late will they be?

My boss approaches,
asks if I'm working today.
Are they serious?

No, I just really
like sitting outside this store
at seven a.m.

A VISIT TO BIZARRO WORLD

Boss gave me award
for great customer service.
I'm so confused now.

My boss just offered
to run and fetch me donuts.
What's happening here?

Boss told co-worker
that she should be more like me.
This is not a joke.

REGRETS, PART TWO

The new boss cries out,
"Shouldn't have taken this job!"
I reply, "Well, yeah."

She then says to me,
"You should be the manager."
Cue endless laughter.

Yeah...I know better
than to be a manager
at this company.

YOU WON'T LIKE THE STOCK GIRL WHEN SHE'S ANGRY

Message for my boss:
Don't bother sucking up now.
It will not help you.

My boss wants to know
why I'm so damn mad at her.
Where do I begin?

Remember that time
you screwed me over big time?
Yeah? Well, so do I.

BOSS BATTLE

Watching bosses fight
o'er vacation schedules
out on the sales floor.

Their angry voices,
red faces, and shaking fists
greet all who enter.

Welcome to the store!
Come for the sales and stay for
the public fighting!

Maybe you shouldn't
fight in front of customers?
Just thinking out loud.

UNNECESSARY REMINDER

I do remember
how a hanger works, but thanks
for the reminder.

Love it when my boss
talks to me like I haven't
worked here for ten years.

Yes, those two haiku
were chock full of sarcasm.
So glad you noticed.

HUG

Boss wants to hug me.
No no no no no no no
no no no no no.

No no no no no
no no no no no no
no no no no no.

What is wrong with you?
Why did you ever think that
I'd want to hug you?

You do not like me,
and I don't like you, either.
What's with the hugging?

HAVE RED PEN.
WILL CORRECT GRAMMAR.

Fixing poor grammar
in my boss's to-do list
using a red pen.

Takes me a while
to figure out exactly
what 'manakin' is.

She's not using the
correct form of their/they're/there.
I think I may cry.

HARD PASS

My boss would like me
to come in on my day off
to mop the sales floor.

Ha ha ha ha ha
ha ha ha ha ha ha ha
ha ha ha ha ha.

Ha ha ha ha ha
ha ha ha ha ha ha ha
ha ha ha yeah, no.

BRIBES, PART TWO

For crying out loud,
stop trying to bribe me and
just do your damn job!

Never seen someone
work so damn hard to avoid
doing any work.

THIS ONE'S ON YOU

When you send two texts
saying DO NOT COME TO WORK,
I won't go to work.

It is then unfair
for you to call and ask me
why I'm not at work.

Also, it's stupid
to be open in this storm.
Just close the damn store.

Nothing we sell is
vital enough to merit
being there right now.

WHAT'S IN A NAME?

For some weird reason,
the boss thinks my name's Barbie,
and yet it isn't.

May I direct your
attention to the nametag
you force me to wear?

However, I do
admire your commitment
to being so wrong.

BEST OF THE REST

In a stand-off with
my boss over something dumb.
It must be Monday.

It's pretty bad when
I must tell the boss to be
nicer to people.

When boss assigns task,
then cackles like a villain,
be very afraid.

I love how my boss
feels the need to thank me for
showing up each shift.

THE BREAKROOM

SETTING THE SCENE

The breakroom table—
center of snacks and gossip.
Oh, how I hate it.

Someone left Kit Kats
out on the breakroom table.
You know what that means…

Any food left out
on the breakroom table is
community food.

BREAKTIME GUIDELINES

I am on a break.
Why do you insist upon
talking to me here?

You may talk to me
during my lunch breaks only
if I'm on fire.

Or if the building
happens to be on fire,
feel free to tell me.

Otherwise, you should
refrain from speaking to me
when I'm sitting here.

ODE TO DONUTS

Donuts are the best.
I like donuts so much more
than my co-workers.

Delicious deep-fried
rings of outstanding flavor
and carbs and sugar!

They make my day here
so much more tolerable,
unlike co-workers.

CHEETOS

Someone left Cheetos
out on the breakroom table.
Think I shall eat them.

There's nothing like that
neon orange crunchiness
to start off one's day.

Basho never wrote
any poems about Cheetos.
I feel bad for him.

SHAKE STEALING, PART ONE

It seems someone took
my protein shake from the fridge.
We are not amused.

Everyone knows that
food abandoned on table
is fair game for all.

But my protein shake
was in fridge clearly labeled,
and not with your name.

DONUT DILEMMA

Boss brought in donuts.
Torn between love of donuts
and dislike of her.

This is so unfair.
Knowing they're there just taunts me.
I must remain strong.

Eating donuts and
trying to convince myself
my boss did not win.

CHOCOLATE CAKE

I've been left alone
with a chocolate sheet cake.
Challenge accepted.

Walk by breakroom and
steal a slice, then another...
Soon cake is half gone.

This job is hard work.
I require lots of cake
to keep me going.

I'm so full of cake,
I see a sugar coma
in my near future.

SHAKE STEALING, PART TWO

Seriously, now.
Stop stealing my protein shakes!
Why are you like this?

That protein shake is—
say it with me—MINE, not yours,
so stop stealing it.

You so will not like
a protein-deprived stock girl.
I promise you that.

BEST OF THE REST

Ate your Doritos.
I'm not sorry I did it.
They were delicious.

Peanut butter cups
have protein in them, therefore
they're a healthy snack.

Cheetos and Kit Kats:
the breakfast of champions
and surly stock girls.

How many haiku
can I write about donuts?
We may never know…

MY ACTUAL JOB

SO IT BEGINS

I'd enjoy morning
so much more if it started
later in the day.

Heading off to work.
Sometimes I think this job will
be the death of me.

Start of a new shift.
Wonder what excitement will
bypass me this time.

Working in retail
always makes me so glad I
bothered with college.

TRUE STORY

It's true that I have
a terrible attitude.
Good thing I don't care.

However, I have
an excellent work ethic.
It balances out.

Which is good because,
otherwise, there'd be no need
to keep me around.

CARDBOARD KINGDOM

Boxes everywhere!
So many that I forget
what the sun looks like.

Oh, wall of cardboard,
do you never shrink in size?
Please stop mocking me.

Cardboard avalanche,
and I am trapped underneath
while co-workers laugh.

WHAT'S IN THE BOX?

A box labeled 'heads'
arrived at the store today.
Scared to open it…

Box marked 'stds'
arrived at the store today.
Think I'll leave it closed.

Looking at a box
someone marked 'butt cardigans'.
Commence hysterics.

Labeling boxes
in Russian until people
stop annoying me.

A DAY IN THE LIFE

Hanging outerwear
and later, I'll hang some more.
The fun never starts.

I don't know why, but
the new henley shirts smell bad.
Where's my hazmat suit?

Flannel has arrived.
Shirts and pajama bottoms
everywhere you look.

I despise flannel.
I am drowning in the stuff.
Death to all flannel.

CHRISTMAS IN OCTOBER

Christmas music has
started playing at the store.
I think I may cry.

It is Halloween.
It is way too early for
holiday music.

The music repeats
every two damn hours, and
my shift lasts for six.

Singing along with
the Christmas music CD.
Someone kill me now.

CHRISTMAS IN OCTOBER
(CONTINUED)

I refuse to have
a holly jolly Christmas
before December.

Santa ain't coming
for another two damn months.
Play another song.

I won't rock around
the Christmas anything, and
you cannot make me.

SLEIGH RIDE SATIATION

How many versions
of 'Sleigh Ride' does one CD
really need to have?

The answer is one,
in case you were curious.
Certainly not four.

It's not like there's a
shortage of Christmas music
from which you could choose.

FALLING MOTIVATION, PART ONE

Just been informed that
I do not qualify for
further pay raises.

A stock girl is worth
only so much an hour,
and I've reached that mark.

Find it hard to care
about my job performance
in wake of this news.

UNEXPECTED GUEST

That moment when the
store doors are open and a
skunk comes strolling in…

See customers flee
as the skunk makes its way down
the center aisle.

Sorry, management,
dealing with wildlife is
above my pay grade.

UNEXPECTED GUEST
(CONTINUED)

The skunk seems to be
sleeping with the mannequins
in the front window.

How come everyone
who isn't me gets to take
a nap in this store?

Now newly refreshed,
the skunk heads back out again…
and I close the doors.

RULES TO LIVE BY

Best not to startle
the stock girl on the ladder.
It makes her fall down.

Beware the stock girl
who has gone deathly silent.
Nothing good follows.

EMPLOYEE OF THE MONTH?

Just found out I was
named employee of the month...
seven months ago.

I have two questions:
Why didn't you tell me, and
why would you pick me?

Exactly how bad
was the rest of the staff that
you chose me for this?

INVENTORY TIME

Inventory prep
is the most boring job on
the face of the earth.

Counting pairs of socks
and wishing that people had
stolen more of them.

One, two, three, four, five.
Today's shift is brought to you
by *Sesame Street*.

Why do you insist
on talking to me when I'm
trying to count shirts?

INVENTORY TIME
(CONTINUED)

Whose idea was it
to do inventory on
Superbowl Sunday?

Inventory teams
never seem capable of
counting correctly.

They're supposed to be
the specialists here and yet
they really are…not.

Would it be okay
if I did it all myself
while you wait outside?

STAFF MEETING

Time for most boring
ritual of retail life:
dreaded staff meeting…

Endless litany
of sales numbers and reports.
My eyes glaze over.

Practicing techniques
to sell clothes to customers
that I'll never use.

Boss trying so hard
to hype up the company's
new dumb strategies.

STAFF MEETING
(CONTINUED)

Separated from
co-worker at staff meeting
for laughing too much.

Staff meetings are meant
to be serious affairs.
No laughing allowed.

It doesn't matter
that the topic at hand is
so ridiculous.

It's cute how my boss
thinks I won't just keep laughing,
even when alone.

LUNCHUS INTERRUPTUS

Pulled away from lunch
to help a woman pick out
a new set of sheets.

I'm happy to help.
Having a hot lunch is just
so overrated.

It isn't as though
anybody else works here,
or something like that.

I mean, there's no way
you could have helped that woman
all by your lonesome.

EMPLOYEE HANDBOOK

Bang head against wall.
Repeat until you forget
that you still work here.

Abandon all hope
all ye who work at this store,
where joy goes to die.

TRAINING

I've been asked to show
the new manager how to
do their job today.

Lesson number one:
The stock girl is never wrong;
you are never right.

Lesson number two:
Annoying the stock girl is
such a bad idea.

Lesson number three:
It's always best to just leave
the stock girl alone.

PA ANNOUNCEMENT

Boss wants me to write
announcement for the shoppers.
How about: "Go home"?

"No, something nicer,"
she says, so then I suggest,
"Please get the hell out."

"Never mind," she says.
"I'll just figure out something
to say by myself."

A GIFT AND A CURSE

Precision folding
is such a stupid talent.
Wish I could juggle.

Shake out pair of jeans,
refold with exact edges
and uniform curves.

Build perfect stacks of
perfectly folded denim.
Repeat until done.

Precision folding
the denim wall takes *hours*.
Please stop touching it.

A GIFT AND A CURSE
(CONTINUED)

My boss says to me,
"Not everybody can fold
as well as you do."

I know that too well.
I've witnessed my co-workers
suck at it for years.

But they sure do love
standing around to watch me
fold all of these jeans.

Which is not at all
really weird and annoying.
Except that it is.

BREAKING POINT

I cannot deal with
the rampant incompetence
infesting this store.

Where's an asteroid
when you need it to destroy
the place where you work?

AUDIENCE

A customer stops
to watch me precision fold
the men's denim wall.

He then tells me that
I'm the most perfect folder
in the whole damn world.

Thanks for noticing
my remarkable skill set.
It's a dream come true.

WELCOME IN

Thank you for coming
during our big annual
bed pillow event…

where shoppers can save
so much money on pillows
they don't even want!

Now may I request
that you take a pillow and
smother me with it?

PHONE FAIL

That moment when you
answer the phone but forget
where it is you work.

Thank you for calling...
wherever the hell I am.
How may I help you?

FALLING MOTIVATION, PART TWO

Without a warning,
motivational poster
falls onto the floor.

Sadly, it would seem
I lack the motivation
to pick it back up.

I suppose this means
motivational poster
may be defective.

CAN'T BELIEVE I MISSED IT

I leave for a week
and store catches on fire.
There's a lesson here.

Might be a good thing
I was in another state
when this happened, though…

BACK FROM VACATION

I leave for a week
and delivery guy cries
when he sees I'm back.

"No one else knows how
to do your damn job," he says.
"Don't leave me again!"

BEST OF THE REST

I am like a shark
who never stops moving through
this cardboard ocean.

I think the time clock
is really moving backwards.
This shift will not end.

It's time to punch out
and run screaming for the hills.
See you next time, kids!

ACKNOWLEDGEMENTS

I would like to thank
my family and my friends.
You're awesome people!

Thank you to Ralph Dahle,
the Poet Laureate of
Melbourne Beach writers.

Your idea helped me
figure out just how to put
this book together.

Thank you to Chrys Fey,
whose input on this project
was invaluable.

And last, but not least,
thank you to the people who
inspired these poems.

If you hadn't been
so…entertaining, this book
would not exist now.

ABOUT THE AUTHOR

Some anxiety
in a trench coat pretending
to be a person.

Raised in New England,
now living in Florida.
Writes stories and poems.

She loves her puppies,
notebooks, stickers, purple pens,
swords and sarcasm.

You can visit her
at mjfifield.com,
if you're so inclined.

www.ingramcontent.com/pod-product-compliance
Lightning Source LLC
Chambersburg PA
CBHW060326050426
42449CB00011B/2670